M000035054

*To sum up, each one of you is to love
his wife as himself,
and the wife is to respect her husband.*

—

Ephesians 5:33 Holman CSB

20 THINGS

I NEED TO TELL MY HUSBAND

©2009 Freeman-Smith, LLC.
All rights reserved. Except for brief quotations used in reviews, articles, or other media, no part of this book may be reproduced or transmitted in any form or by any means, electronic or mechanical, including photocopying, recording, or by information storage or retrieval system, without permission by the publisher.
Freeman-Smith, LLC.
Nashville, TN 37202

The quoted ideas expressed in this book (but not Scripture verses) are not, in all cases, exact quotations, as some have been edited for clarity and brevity. In all cases, the author has attempted to maintain the speaker's original intent. In some cases, quoted material for this book was obtained from secondary sources, primarily print media. While every effort was made to ensure the accuracy of these sources, the accuracy cannot be guaranteed. For additions, deletions, corrections, or clarifications in future editions of this text, please write Freeman-Smith, LLC.

The Holy Bible, King James Version

The Holy Bible, New King James Version (NKJV) Copyright © 1982 by Thomas Nelson, Inc. Used by permission.

New Century Version®. (NCV) Copyright © 1987, 1988, 1991 by Word Publishing, a division of Thomas Nelson, Inc. All rights reserved. Used by permission.

The Holman Christian Standard Bible™ (Holman CSB) Copyright © 1999, 2000, 2001 by Holman Bible Publishers. Used by permission.

The Holy Bible, New International Version®. (NIV) Copyright © 1973, 1978, 1984 International Bible Society. Used by permission of Zondervan. All rights reserved.

The Holy Bible. New Living Translation (NLT) copyright © 1996 Tyndale Charitable Trust. Used by permission of Tyndale House Publishers.

The New American Standard Bible®, (NASB) Copyright © 1960, 1962, 1963, 1968, 1971, 1972, 1973, 1975, 1977, 1995 by The Lockman Foundation. Used by permission.

Scripture taken from The Message. (MSG) Copyright © 1993, 1994, 1995, 1996, 2000, 2001, 2002. Used by permission of NavPress Publishing Group.

Cover Design by Kim Russell / Wahoo Designs
Page Layout by Bart Dawson

ISBN 978-1-60587-108-0

Printed in the United States of America

20 THINGS
I NEED TO TELL
MY
HUSBAND

INDEX OF TOPICS

INTRODUCTION

"**B**ut the greatest of these is love"— seven familiar words that remind us of a simple truth: God places a high priority on love . . . and so should we. Faith is important, of course. So too is hope. But love is more important still.

Considering all the wonderful things your husband has done for you, you may have a few things to say to him. You may want to express your love, your admiration, your thanks, or your faithfulness. And if you'd like to communicate all these things and more, then the ideas in this book can help.

This text contains 20 things that every wife needs to tell her husband. If you sincerely wish to make your marriage flourish, take these ideas, put them into your own words, and express them to your husband. And while you're at it, please remember that it isn't enough to simply talk about these principles; you must also weave them into the fabric of your marriage. When you do, you'll learn firsthand the truth of God's Word: "the greatest of these" is now—and will forever be—the love that is shared between you and your husband.

"I LOVE YOU NOW AND FOREVER."

Now these three remain:
faith, hope, and love.
But the greatest of these is love.

—

1 Corinthians 13:13 Holman CSB

Because you are a thoughtful woman and a caring wife, you understand the crucial role that love does play—and should play—in every marriage, including your own. And the familiar words of 1st Corinthians 13 serve as a beautiful reminder of the importance and the power of love.

Christ showed His love for us on the cross, and as Christians we are called to return Christ's love by sharing it.

Sometimes, of course, love is easy (puppies and sleeping children come to mind), and sometimes love is hard (imperfect spouses come to mind). But God's Word is clear: We are to love our spouses at all times, not just when they seem most lovable.

So do the right thing: Tell your husband that you love him every chance you get. Nurture him; praise him; express your admiration for him, and give him encouragement. Demonstrate your love with words and deeds—your husband needs both. And he deserves both.

Above all, keep your love for one another at full strength, since love covers a multitude of sins.

1 Peter 4:8 Holman CSB

If I speak the languages of men and of angels, but do not have love, I am a sounding gong or a clanging cymbal.

1 Corinthians 13:1 Holman CSB

Love one another earnestly from a pure heart.

1 Peter 1:22 Holman CSB

Now the goal of our instruction is love from a pure heart, a good conscience, and a sincere faith.

1 Timothy 1:5 Holman CSB

The one who does not love does not know God, because God is love.

1 John 4:8 Holman CSB

More Great Ideas

Marriage should be many hours of joy interrupted by an occasional minute or two of frustration—not the other way around.

Marie T. Freeman

The first natural tie of human society is man and wife.

St. Augustine

Joy is love exalted; peace is love in repose; gentleness is love in society; goodness is love in action; faith is love on the battlefield; meekness is love in school; and temperance is love in training.

D. L. Moody

Only a love that has no regard for vessels and jars—appearances or image—only a love that will lavish its most treasured essence on the feet of Jesus can produce the kind of fragrance that draws cynics and believers alike into His presence.

Gloria Gaither

Line by line, moment by moment, special times are etched into our memories in the permanent ink of everlasting love in our relationships.

Gloria Gaither

Love is an attribute of God. To love others is evidence of a genuine faith.

Kay Arthur

Suppose that I understand the Bible. And, suppose that I am the greatest preacher who ever lived! The Apostle Paul wrote that unless I have love, "I am nothing."

Billy Graham

Affection should be the underlying atmosphere of marriage twenty-four hours a day, seven days a week.

Ed Young

A TIMELY TIP

You should only say "I love you" on the days that end in "y."

YOUR HUSBAND, YOUR BEST FRIEND

A man leaves his father and mother and bonds with his wife, and they become one flesh.
Genesis 2:24 Holman CSB

Here's a time-tested prescription for a blissfully happy marriage: make certain that your spouse is your best friend.

Genuine friendship between a husband and wife should be treasured and nurtured. As Christians, we are commanded to love one another.

Is your husband your best friend? If so, you are immensely blessed by God—never take this gift for granted. So today, remember the important role that friendship plays in your marriage. That friendship is, after all, a glorious gift, praised by God. Give thanks for that gift and nurture it.

YOUR OWN IDEAS ABOUT:
Ways to Express the Love You Feel for Your Husband

_____

_____

_____

_____

_____

_____

_____

_____

_____

_____

_____

_____

_____

"I WILL HONOR YOU BY PUTTING GOD FIRST IN MY LIFE."

You shall have no other gods before Me.

—

Exodus 20:3 NKJV

D o you and your husband put God first in your marriage? Or do you allow yourselves to be hijacked by the inevitable obligations and distractions of 21st-century life? When you and your beloved allow Christ to reign over your lives and your marriage, your household will be eternally blessed.

God loved this world so much that He sent His Son to save it. And now only one real question remains: what will you and yours do in response to God's love? The answer should be obvious: You must put God first in every aspect of your lives, including your marriage.

God is with you always, listening to your thoughts and prayers, watching over your every move. As the demands of everyday life weigh down upon you, you may be tempted to ignore God's presence or—worse yet—to rebel against His commandments. But, when you quiet yourself and acknowledge His presence, God touches your heart and restores your spirits.

At this very moment, God is seeking to work in you and through you. So why not let Him do it right now?

Be careful not to forget the Lord.

Deuteronomy 6:12 Holman CSB

It is good to give thanks to the Lord, and to sing praises to Your name, O Most High; to declare Your lovingkindness in the morning, and Your faithfulness every night.

Psalm 92:1-2 NKJV

Love the Lord your God with all your heart, with all your soul, and with all your strength.

Deuteronomy 6:5 Holman CSB

The Devil said to Him, "I will give You their splendor and all this authority, because it has been given over to me, and I can give it to anyone I want. If You, then, will worship me, all will be Yours." And Jesus answered him, "It is written: You shall worship the Lord your God, and Him alone you shall serve."

Luke 4:6-8 Holman CSB

For where your treasure is, there your heart will be also.

Luke 12:34 Holman CSB

MORE GREAT IDEAS

If God has the power to create and sustain the universe, He is more than able to sustain your marriage and your ministry, your faith and your finances, your hope and your health.

Anne Graham Lotz

Love has its source in God, for love is the very essence of His being.

Kay Arthur

It is when we come to the Lord in our nothingness, our powerlessness and our helplessness that He then enables us to love in a way which, without Him, would be absolutely impossible.

Elisabeth Elliot

Marriage is God's idea. He "crafted" it. If your marriage is broken, all the "repairmen" or counselors or seminars you take it to will be unable to fix it; take it to Him. The Creator who made it in the first place can make it work again.

Anne Graham Lotz

When I have learnt to love God better than my earthly dearest, I shall love my earthly dearest better than I do now. When first things are put first, second things are not suppressed but increased.

C. S. Lewis

Oh, that we might discern the will of God, surrender to His calling, resign the masses of activities, and do a few things well. What a legacy that would be for our children.

Beth Moore

The love life of the Christian is a crucial battleground. There, if nowhere else, it will be determined who is Lord: the world, the self, and the devil—or the Lord Christ.

Elisabeth Elliot

A Timely Tip

Today, spend time talking to your husband about the role that God does play—and should play—in your marriage.

MORE FROM GOD'S WORD ABOUT FEAR OF GOD

Don't consider yourself to be wise; fear the Lord and turn away from evil.

Proverbs 3:7 Holman CSB

The fear of the Lord is the beginning of knowledge, but fools despise wisdom and instruction.

Proverbs 1:7 NKJV

To fear the Lord is to hate evil.

Proverbs 8:13 Holman CSB

The fear of the Lord is the beginning of wisdom, and the knowledge of the Holy One is understanding.

Proverbs 9:10 Holman CSB

The fear of the Lord is the beginning of wisdom; all who follow His instructions have good insight.

Psalm 111:10 Holman CSB

23

YOUR OWN IDEAS ABOUT:
Ways to Put God First in Your Marriage

_____

_____

_____

_____

_____

_____

_____

_____

_____

_____

_____

_____

_____

_____

"I THANK YOU FOR YOUR PRAYERS, AND I WILL NEVER STOP PRAYING FOR YOU."

The intense prayer of the righteous is very powerful.

—

James 5:16 Holman CSB

Is prayer an integral part of your married life or is it a hit-or-miss habit? Do you and your husband "pray without ceasing," or is prayer usually an afterthought? Do you regularly pray together, or do you only bow your heads in unison during Sunday morning services? The answers to these questions will determine the quality of your prayer life and, to a surprising extent, the spiritual strength of your marriage.

Andrew Murray observed, "Some people pray just to pray, and some people pray to know God." Your task, along with your husband, is to pray together, not out of habit or obligation, but out of a sincere desire to know your Heavenly Father.

Through constant prayers, you and your husband should petition God, you should praise God, and you should seek God's guidance for your marriage and your life.

Prayer changes things, prayer changes people, and prayer changes marriages. So don't limit your prayers to meals or to bedtime. Pray constantly about things great and small. God is listening, and He wants to hear from you—and your spouse—right now.

If you really carry out the royal law prescribed in Scripture, You shall love your neighbor as yourself, you are doing well.

James 2:8 Holman CSB

Therefore I want the men in every place to pray, lifting up holy hands without anger or argument.

1 Timothy 2:8 Holman CSB

And let us not grow weary while doing good, for in due season we shall reap if we do not lose heart.

Galatians 6:9 NKJV

And whenever you stand praying, if you have anything against anyone, forgive him, that your Father in heaven may also forgive you your trespasses.

Mark 11:25 NKJV

Rejoice in hope; be patient in affliction; be persistent in prayer.

Romans 12:12 Holman CSB

More Great Ideas

The hard part about being a praying wife is maintaining a pure heart. If you have resentment, anger, unforgiveness, or an ungodly attitude—even if there's good reason for it—you'll have a difficult time seeing answers to your prayers. But if you can release those feelings to God in total honesty, there is nothing that can change a marriage more dramatically.

Stormie Omartian

As we join together in prayer, we draw on God's enabling might in a way that multiplies our own efforts many times over.

Shirley Dobson

In souls filled with love, the desire to please God is continual prayer.

John Wesley

Prayer is the ultimate love language. It communicates in ways we can't.

Stormie Omartian

We must lay before Him what is in us, not what ought to be in us.

C. S. Lewis

Jesus practiced secret prayer and asked us to follow His example.

Catherine Marshall

Our prayer must not be self-centered. It must arise not only because we feel our own need as a burden we must lay upon God, but also because we are so bound up in love for our fellow men that we feel their needs as acutely as our own. To make intercession for men is the most powerful and practical way in which we can express our love for them.

John Calvin

A TIMELY TIP

Today, think about your family's prayer life. Are you really in touch with God? If so, keep it up; if not, talk to your spouse about the need to carve out more time with God.

More from God's Word About Silence

Be still, and know that I am God.

Psalm 46:10 NKJV

Be silent before the Lord and wait expectantly for Him.

Psalm 37:7 Holman CSB

In quietness and confidence shall be your strength.

Isaiah 30:15 NKJV

I am not alone, because the Father is with Me.

John 16:32 Holman CSB

Draw near to God, and He will draw near to you.

James 4:8 Holman CSB

YOUR OWN IDEAS ABOUT:
The Importance of Prayer

_____

_____

_____

_____

_____

_____

_____

_____

_____

_____

_____

_____

_____

_____

_____

_____

_____

"I AM COMMITTED TO OUR MARRIAGE."

So they are no longer two, but one flesh.
Therefore what God has joined together,
man must not separate.

—

Matthew 19:6 Holman CSB

In a good marriage, the words "love" and "commitment" are intertwined. According to God, genuine love is patient, unselfish, and kind, but it's goes beyond that—genuine love is committed love, and that means that genuine love is more than a feeling . . . it is a decision to make love endure, no matter what.

Unfortunately, we live in a world where marriage vows are sometimes taken far too lightly. Too many couples are far too quick to push the panic button—or the eject button—and the results are predictably tragic.

As a married woman who has vowed to love your husband "till death do you part," you must take that vow very seriously. Your husband must know, beyond any doubt, that you are totally committed to him, totally committed to your family, and totally committed to your marriage. How can you do it? The best place to start is by putting God right where He belongs: at the absolute center of your family and your marriage.

When you and your spouse worship God together, you'll soon notice a change in your relationship. When the two of you sincerely embrace God's love, you will feel differently about yourself, your marriage, your family, and your world. When you and your husband embrace God's love together, your marriage will be transformed. And, when the two of you accept the Father's grace and share His love, you will be blessed here on earth and throughout eternity.

So, if you genuinely seek to build a marriage that will stand the test of time, make God the foundation. When you do, your love will endure for a lifetime and beyond.

To sum up, each one of you is to love his wife as himself, and the wife is to respect her husband.

Ephesians 5:33 Holman CSB

A man leaves his father and mother and bonds with his wife, and they become one flesh.

Genesis 2:24 Holman CSB

A husband should fulfill his marital duty to his wife, and likewise a wife to her husband.

1 Corinthians 7:3 Holman CSB

Wives, be submissive to your husbands, as is fitting in the Lord. Husbands, love your wives and don't become bitter against them.

Colossians 3:18-19 Holman CSB

A virtuous woman is a crown to her husband....

Proverbs 12:4 KJV

MORE GREAT IDEAS

Being committed to one's mate is not a matter of demanding rights, but a matter of releasing rights.

Charles Swindoll

There is nothing wrong with a marriage that sacrifice wouldn't heal.

Elisabeth Elliot

If a husband and wife are deeply committed to Jesus Christ, they enjoy enormous advantages over the family with no spiritual dimension.

James Dobson

A beautiful relationship with your mate will enhance your creativity and upgrade your standard of living while improving your quality of life.

Zig Ziglar

They [Billy and Ruth Graham] not only share a deep love for one another, but a mutual respect.

Gigi Graham Tchividjian

The institution of marriage has been a sacred bond of fidelity between a man and a woman in every culture throughout recorded history. The pledge of loyalty and mutual support represented by marriage vows is a promise of commitment that extends to every aspect of life.

James Dobson

How committed are you to breaking the ice of prayerlessness so that you and your mate can seek the Lord openly and honestly together, releasing control over your marriage into the capable, trustworthy, but often surprising hands of God?

Stormie Omartian

A TIMELY TIP

Commitment first! The best marriages are built upon an unwavering commitment to God and an unwavering commitment to your husband. So, if you're totally committed, congratulations; if you're not, you're building your marriage (and your life) on a very shaky foundation.

A Marriage Built on Trust

*Honor marriage, and guard the sacredness of
sexual intimacy between wife and husband.
God draws a firm line against casual and illicit sex.*

Hebrews 13:4 MSG

The best relationships—and the best marriages—are built upon a foundation of honesty and trust. Without trust, marriages soon begin to wither; with trust, marriages soon begin to flourish.

For Christian men and women, honesty is the right policy because it's God's policy. God's Word makes it clear: "Lying lips are an abomination to the Lord, but those who deal truthfully are His delight" (Proverbs 12:22 NKJV).

Sometimes, honesty is difficult; sometimes, honesty is painful; sometimes, honesty makes us feel uncomfortable. Despite these temporary feelings of discomfort, we must make honesty the hallmark of all our relationships; otherwise, we invite needless suffering into our own lives and into the lives of those we love.

Do you want your love to last forever? Then you and your husband must build a marriage based upon mutual trust and unerring truth. Both of you deserve nothing less . . . and neither, for that matter, does God.

The one who lives with integrity lives securely, but whoever perverts his ways will be found out.

Proverbs 10:9 Holman CSB

The greatest gift you can give your marriage partner is your fidelity. The greatest character trait you can provide your spouse and your family is moral and ethical self-control.

Charles Swindoll

Love is not soft as water is; it is solid as a rock on which the waves of hatred beat in vain.

Corrie ten Boom

Truth becomes hard if it is not softened by love, and love becomes soft if not strengthened by truth.

E. Stanley Jones

My commitment to my marriage vows places me in an utterly unique and profoundly significant relationship with the most important human being on earth—my spouse.

Joni Eareckson Tada

Trust is like "money in the bank" in a marriage. There must be a reasonable amount of it on deposit to ensure the security of a marital union.

Ed Young

Blessed assurance, Jesus is mine! O what a foretaste of glory divine!

Fanny Crosby

We sometimes fear to bring our troubles to God because we think they must seem small to Him. But, if they are large enough to vex and endanger our welfare, they are large enough to touch His heart of love.

R. A. Torrey

YOUR OWN IDEAS ABOUT:
The Importance of Commitment within Your Marriage

_____

_____

_____

_____

_____

_____

_____

_____

_____

_____

_____

_____

_____

_____

"THANK YOU FOR YOUR PATIENCE. I WILL BE PATIENT WITH YOU, TOO."

Love is patient; love is kind.

—

1 Corinthians 13:4 Holman CSB

Marriage is an exercise in patience. From time to time, even if your husband is the most considerate man in the world, he may do things that confound you, or confuse you, or anger you. Why? Because even the most considerate man in the world is still an imperfect human being, capable of missteps, misdeeds, and mistakes. So, because your husband is a fallible-yet-lovable guy, you should learn to be patient with his shortcomings (just as he, too, must be patient with yours).

Are you one of those women who demand perfection from everybody, with the possible exception of yourself? If so, it's time to reassess your expectations. God doesn't expect perfection, and neither should you.

Proverbs 19:11 makes it clear: "People with good sense restrain their anger; they earn esteem by overlooking wrongs" (NLT). So the next time you find yourself drumming your fingers while waiting for your hubby to do the right thing, take a deep breath and ask God for patience. After all, the world unfolds according to God's timetable, not yours. And your loved ones live—and grow—according to their own timetables, too. Sometimes, you must wait patiently, and that's as it should be. After all, think how patient God has been with you.

A patient spirit is better than a proud spirit.

Ecclesiastes 7:8 Holman CSB

Therefore the Lord is waiting to show you mercy, and is rising up to show you compassion, for the Lord is a just God. Happy are all who wait patiently for Him.

Isaiah 30:18 Holman CSB

A patient person [shows] great understanding, but a quick-tempered one promotes foolishness.

Proverbs 14:29 Holman CSB

Rejoice in hope; be patient in affliction; be persistent in prayer.

Romans 12:12 Holman CSB

Patience is better than power, and controlling one's temper, than capturing a city.

Proverbs 16:32 Holman CSB

MORE GREAT IDEAS

Waiting is the hardest kind of work, but God knows best, and we may joyfully leave all in His hands.

Lottie Moon

Waiting is an essential part of spiritual discipline. It can be the ultimate test of faith.

Anne Graham Lotz

By his wisdom, he orders his delays so that they prove to be far better than our hurries.

C. H. Spurgeon

The next time you're disappointed, don't panic. Don't give up. Just be patient and let God remind you he's still in control.

Max Lucado

He makes us wait. He keeps us in the dark on purpose. He makes us walk when we want to run, sit still when we want to walk, for he has things to do in our souls that we are not interested in.

Elisabeth Elliot

God never hurries. There are no deadlines against which He must work. To know this is to quiet our spirits and relax our nerves.

A. W. Tozer

God gave everyone patience—wise people use it.

Anonymous

As we wait on God, He helps us use the winds of adversity to soar above our problems. As the Bible says, "Those who wait on the LORD… shall mount up with wings like eagles."

Billy Graham

A TIMELY TIP

Do you expect your husband to be patient with you? Then your husband has the right to expect the same from you. No exceptions.

MORE FROM GOD'S WORD ABOUT KINDNESS

Just as you want others to do for you, do the same for them.

Luke 6:31 Holman CSB

Finally, all of you be of one mind, having compassion for one another; love as brothers, be tenderhearted, be courteous.

1 Peter 3:8 NKJV

And may the Lord make you increase and abound in love to one another and to all.

1 Thessalonians 3:12 NKJV

And be kind and compassionate to one another, forgiving one another, just as God also forgave you in Christ.

Ephesians 4:32 Holman CSB

Pure and undefiled religion before our God and Father is this: to look after orphans and widows in their distress and to keep oneself unstained by the world.

James 1:27 Holman CSB

47

YOUR OWN IDEAS ABOUT:
The Rewards of Being Patient

_____

_____

_____

_____

_____

_____

_____

_____

_____

_____

_____

_____

_____

_____

_____

"I UNDERSTAND THE IMPORTANCE OF CLEAR, LOVING, OPEN LINES OF COMMUNICATION."

*A word fitly spoken is like
apples of gold in settings of silver.*

—

Proverbs 25:11 NKJV

Your skills as a communicator will have a profound impact upon your relationships, starting with that most important relationship: your marriage. Here are a few simple rules that can help:

1. Think First, Speak Second: If you blurt out the first thing that comes into your head, you may say things that are better left unsaid.

2. Learn to Be a Good Listener: Far too many marriages are unsuccessful because one or both spouses simply don't make the effort to listen. If you want your marriage to flourish, listen carefully to your spouse.

3. Don't Be a Chronic Complainer: You'll never whine your way to a happy marriage, so don't even try.

4. Be a Trustworthy Communicator: Don't hedge the truth, don't omit important facts, and don't make promises that you can't keep.

5. Be Encouraging: You should be your spouse's biggest booster, not your spouse's constant critic.

God's Word reminds us that "Reckless words pierce like a sword, but the tongue of the wise brings healing" (Proverbs 12:18 NIV). So, if you seek to be a source of encouragement to your loved ones, you must measure your words carefully. You must speak wisely, not impulsively. You must use words of kindness and praise, not words of anger or derision. And, you must learn how to be truthful without being cruel.

You have the power to lift your loved ones up or to hold them back. When you learn how to lift them up, you'll soon discover that you've lifted yourself up, too.

The heart of the wise teaches his mouth, and adds learning to his lips.

Proverbs 16:23 NKJV

An ungodly man digs up evil, and it is on his lips like a burning fire.

Proverbs 16:27 NKJV

There is one who speaks rashly, like a piercing sword; but the tongue of the wise [brings] healing.

Proverbs 12:18 Holman CSB

May the words of my mouth and the meditation of my heart be acceptable to You, Lord, my rock and my Redeemer.

Psalm 19:14 Holman CSB

Nevertheless let each one of you in particular so love his own wife as himself, and let the wife see that she respects her husband.

Ephesians 5:33 NKJV

MORE GREAT IDEAS

Some of us seem so anxious about avoiding hell that we forget to celebrate our journey toward heaven.

Philip Yancey

God has a course mapped out for your life, and all the inadequacies in the world will not change His mind. He will be with you every step of the way. And though it may take time, He has a celebration planned for when you cross over the "Red Seas" of your life.

Charles Swindoll

The main joy of heaven will be the heavenly Father greeting us in a time and place of rejoicing, celebration, joy, and great reunion.

Bill Bright

In terms of the parable of the Prodigal Son, repentance is the flight home that leads to joyful celebration. It opens the way to a future, to a relationship restored.

Philip Yancey

Both a good marriage and a bad marriage have moments of struggle, but in a healthy relationship, the husband and wife search for answers and areas of agreement because they love each other.

James Dobson

The fewer words, the better prayer.

Martin Luther

Part of good communication is listening with the eyes as well as with the ears.

Josh McDowell

A Timely Tip

Communication is vital to the health of any marriage. If you're having trouble expressing yourself, don't clam up. Instead, keep trying until you finally get the hang of it.

IT TAKES TIME

So teach us to number our days,
that we may gain a heart of wisdom.
Psalm 90:12 NKJV

It takes time to build a strong marriage . . . lots of time. Yet we live in a world where time seems to be an ever-shrinking commodity as we rush from place to place with seldom a moment to spare.

Has the busy pace of life robbed you of high quality time with your husband? If so, it's time to adjust your priorities. And God can help.

When you fervently ask God to help you prioritize your life, He will give you guidance. When you seek His guidance every day, your Creator will reveal Himself in a variety of ways. As a follower of Christ, you must do no less.

When you allow God to help you organize your day, you'll soon discover that there is ample time for your husband and your family. When you make God a full partner in every aspect of your life, He will lead you along the proper path: His path. When you allow God to reign over

55

your heart, He will honor you with spiritual blessings that are simply too numerous to count. So, as you plan for the day ahead, make God's priorities your priorities. When you do, every other priority will have a tendency to fall neatly into place.

And He said to them, "Take heed and beware of covetousness, for one's life does not consist in the abundance of the things he possesses."

Luke 12:15 NKJV

It is important to know that you have to work to keep love alive; you have to protect it and maintain it, just like you would a delicate flower.

James Dobson

It's sobering to contemplate how much time, effort, sacrifice, compromise, and attention we give to acquiring and increasing our supply of something that is totally insignificant in eternity.

Anne Graham Lotz

YOUR OWN IDEAS ABOUT:
The Importance of Effective Communication within Your Marriage

_____

_____

_____

_____

_____

_____

_____

_____

_____

_____

_____

_____

_____

_____

_____

"THANK YOU FOR BEING FAITHFUL WHEN TIMES ARE TOUGH."

Mighty waters cannot extinguish love;
rivers cannot sweep it away.

—

Song of Solomon 8:7 Holman CSB

L ife is a tapestry of good days and difficult days, with the good days predominating. When times are good, we are tempted to take our blessings for granted. But, when times are tough, we discover precisely what we're made of.

Every marriage, like every life, will encounter days of hardship and pain. It is only then that husbands and wives can discover precisely what their marriage is made of.

When we experience a deeply significant loss, we must learn (once again) to trust God and to trust those who love us most. When we do, we come to understand that our suffering carries with it great potential: the potential for intense personal growth and the potential to add depth and meaning to our relationships.

Are you and your husband enduring tough times? If so, hold tightly to each other and turn your hearts toward God. When you do, you may rest assured that the two of you—plus God—can handle anything that comes your way.

We are pressured in every way but not crushed; we are perplexed but not in despair.

2 Corinthians 4:8 Holman CSB

I called to the Lord in my distress; I called to my God. From His temple He heard my voice.

2 Samuel 22:7 Holman CSB

I will be with you when you pass through the waters . . . when you walk through the fire . . . the flame will not burn you. For I the Lord your God, the Holy One of Israel, and your Savior.

Isaiah 43:2-3 Holman CSB

Consider it a great joy, my brothers, whenever you experience various trials, knowing that the testing of your faith produces endurance. But endurance must do its complete work, so that you may be mature and complete, lacking nothing.

James 1:2-4 Holman CSB

For whatever is born of God overcomes the world. And this is the victory that has overcome the world— our faith.

1 John 5:4 NKJV

MORE GREAT IDEAS

Those who abandon ship the first time it enters a storm miss the calm beyond. And the rougher the storms weathered together, the deeper and stronger real love grows.

Ruth Bell Graham

Real love has staying power. Authentic love is tough love. It refuses to look for ways to run away. It always opts for working through.

Charles Swindoll

Father and Mother lived on the edge of poverty, and yet their contentment was not dependent upon their surroundings. Their relationship to each other and to the Lord gave them strength and happiness.

Corrie ten Boom

As a child of God, rest in the knowledge that your Savior precedes you, and He will walk with you through each experience of your life.

Henry Blackaby

We should not be upset when unexpected and upsetting things happen. God, in his wisdom, means to make something of us which we have not yet attained, and He is dealing with us accordingly.

J. I. Packer

One's attitude toward a handicap determines its impact on his life.

James Dobson

A Timely Tip

If you're having tough times, don't hit the panic button and don't keep everything bottled up inside. Talk things over with your husband, and if necessary, find a counselor you can really trust. A second opinion (or, for that matter, a third, fourth, or fifth opinion) is usually helpful. So if your troubles seem overwhelming, be willing to seek outside help—starting, of course, with your pastor.

MORE FROM GOD'S WORD ABOUT ANXIETY

When you pass through the waters, I will be with you; and through the rivers, they shall not overflow you. When you walk through the fire, you shall not be burned, nor shall the flame scorch you. For I am the Lord your God, The Holy One of Israel, your Savior.

Isaiah 43:2-3 NKJV

Be anxious for nothing, but in everything by prayer and supplication with thanksgiving let your requests be made known to God.

Philippians 4:6 NASB

Let not your heart be troubled: ye believe in God, believe also in me.

John 14:1 KJV

Therefore don't worry about tomorrow, because tomorrow will worry about itself. Each day has enough trouble of its own.

Matthew 6:34 Holman CSB

Strengthening Your Marriage with Positive Thoughts

Finally brothers, whatever is true, whatever is honorable, whatever is just, whatever is pure, whatever is lovely, whatever is commendable— if there is any moral excellence and if there is any praise—dwell on these things.
Philippians 4:8 Holman CSB

Have you formed the habit of thinking positive thoughts? Hopefully so, because it's a wonderful way to strengthen your marriage. Once you learn to think positively about your world, your husband, and yourself, you then put the self-fulfilling prophecy to work for you. Because you expect the best, you are much more likely to achieve the best.

You can control, to a surprising extent, the quality, the tone, and the direction of your thoughts. You can learn to prune out the negative ones and let the positive ones flourish. And that's precisely what you should learn to do.

Are you excited about the opportunities of today and thrilled by the possibilities of tomorrow? Do you confidently expect God to lead you to a place of abundance, peace, and joy? And, when your days on earth are over, do you expect to receive the priceless gift of eternal life? If you trust God's promises, and if you have welcomed God's Son into your heart, then you believe that your future is intensely and eternally bright.

Today, as you and your husband prepare to meet the duties of everyday life, pause and consider God's promises. And then think for a moment about the wonderful future that awaits all believers, including both of you. God has promised that your future is secure. Trust that promise, and celebrate the abundance and eternal joy that is now yours through Christ.

Set your minds on what is above,
not on what is on the earth.
Colossians 3:2 Holman CSB

The things we think are the things that feed our souls. If we think on pure and lovely things, we shall grow pure and lovely like them; and the converse is equally true.

Hannah Whitall Smith

No matter how little we can change about our circumstances, we always have a choice about our attitude toward the situation.

Vonette Bright

Whether we think of, or speak to, God, whether we act or suffer for him, all is prayer when we have no other object than his love and the desire of pleasing him.

John Wesley

Your thoughts are the determining factor as to whose mold you are conformed to. Control your thoughts and you control the direction of your life.

Charles Stanley

YOUR OWN IDEAS ABOUT:
How You and Your Husband Deal with Adversity

_____

_____

_____

_____

_____

_____

_____

_____

_____

_____

_____

_____

_____

_____

_____

_____

"I THANK GOD FOR OUR MARRIAGE."

Give thanks to the Lord, for He is good;
His faithful love endures forever.

—

Psalm 118:29 Holman CSB

Your life and your marriage are gifts from God: celebrate those blessings and give thanks. And make no mistake: When you celebrate the gifts of life and love, your thankful heart will serve as a powerful blessing to your husband.

Every good gift comes from God. As believers who have been saved by a risen Christ, we owe unending thanksgiving to our Heavenly Father. Yet sometimes, amid the crush of everyday living, we simply don't stop long enough to pause and thank our Creator for His countless blessings. As Christians, we are blessed beyond measure. Thus, thanksgiving should become a habit, a regular part of our daily routines.

Thoughtful believers can face the inevitable challenges of married life armed with the joy of Christ and the promise of salvation. So whatever this day holds for you, begin it and end it with God as your partner and Christ as your Savior. And throughout the day, give thanks to the One who created you and saved you. Place God squarely at the center of your marriage and your life. Then celebrate! God's love for you is infinite. Accept it joyously and be thankful.

Give thanks to the Lord, for He is good; His faithful love endures forever.

Psalm 118:29 Holman CSB

I will give You thanks with all my heart.

Psalm 138:1 Holman CSB

And whatever you do, in word or in deed, do everything in the name of the Lord Jesus, giving thanks to God the Father through Him.

Colossians 3:17 Holman CSB

Therefore as you have received Christ Jesus the Lord, walk in Him, rooted and built up in Him and established in the faith, just as you were taught, and overflowing with thankfulness.

Colossians 2:6-7 Holman CSB

Thanks be to God for His indescribable gift.

2 Corinthians 9:15 Holman CSB

MORE GREAT IDEAS

God has promised that if we harvest well with the tools of thanksgiving, there will be seeds for planting in the spring.

Gloria Gaither

It is always possible to be thankful for what is given rather than to complain about what is not given. One or the other becomes a habit of life.

Elisabeth Elliot

A friend is one who makes me do my best.

Oswald Chambers

The joy of the Holy Spirit is experienced by giving thanks in all situations.

Bill Bright

Thank God every morning when you get up that you have something to do that day which must be done, whether you like it or not.

Charles Kingsley

Praise and thank God for who He is and for what He has done for you.

Billy Graham

The words "thank" and "think" come from the same root word. If we would think more, we would thank more.

Warren Wiersbe

God often keeps us on the path by guiding us through the counsel of friends and trusted spiritual advisors.

Bill Hybels

A TIMELY TIP

Since you're thankful to the Creator, tell Him so. And keep telling Him so every day of your life.

MORE FROM GOD'S WORD ABOUT WORSHIP

I rejoiced with those who said to me, "Let us go to the house of the Lord."

Psalm 122:1 Holman CSB

And every day they devoted themselves to meeting together in the temple complex, and broke bread from house to house. They ate their food with gladness and simplicity of heart, praising God and having favor with all the people. And every day the Lord added those being saved to them.

Acts 2:46-47 Holman CSB

But an hour is coming, and is now here, when the true worshipers will worship the Father in spirit and truth. Yes, the Father wants such people to worship Him. God is Spirit, and those who worship Him must worship in spirit and truth.

John 4:23-24 Holman CSB

For where two or three are gathered together in My name, I am there among them.

Matthew 18:20 Holman CSB

YOUR OWN IDEAS ABOUT:
Some of the Many Reasons You're Thankful for Your Marriage

_____

_____

_____

_____

_____

_____

_____

_____

_____

_____

_____

_____

_____

_____

_____

"THANK YOU FOR YOUR INTEGRITY. IT ENRICHES OUR MARRIAGE."

Lead a quiet and peaceable life in all godliness and honesty.

—

1 Timothy 2:2 KJV

The best marriages are built upon a firm foundation of honesty and trust. Temporary relationships are built upon the shifting sands of deception and insincerity. Which foundation will you choose?

It has been said on many occasions that honesty is the best policy. But for Christians, it is far more important to note that honesty is God's policy. And if we are to be servants worthy of our Savior, we must be honest and forthright in all our communications with others.

Sometimes, honesty is difficult; sometimes, honesty is painful; sometimes, honesty makes us feel uncomfortable. Despite these temporary feelings of discomfort, we must make honesty the hallmark of all our relationships; otherwise, we invite needless suffering into our own lives and into the lives of those we love.

Sometime soon, perhaps even today, you will be tempted to bend the truth or to break it. Resist that temptation. Truth is God's way… and it must be your way, too.

A woman who fears the Lord will be praised.

Proverbs 31:30 Holman CSB

A good name is to be chosen rather than great riches, loving favor rather than silver and gold.

Proverbs 22:1 NKJV

Do not be deceived: "Evil company corrupts good habits."

1 Corinthians 15:33 NKJV

In all things showing yourself to be a pattern of good works; in doctrine showing integrity, reverence, incorruptibility . . . .

Titus 2:7 NKJV

Let integrity and uprightness preserve me, for I wait for You.

Psalm 25:21 NKJV

More Great Ideas

The trials of life can be God's tools for engraving His image on our character.

Warren Wiersbe

There is no way to grow a saint overnight. Character, like the oak tree, does not spring up like a mushroom.

Vance Havner

In matters of style, swim with the current. In matters of principle, stand like a rock.

Thomas Jefferson

Each one of us is God's special work of art. Through us, He teaches and inspires, delights and encourages, informs and uplifts all those who view our lives. God, the master artist, is most concerned about expressing Himself—His thoughts and His intentions—through what He paints in our characters.

Joni Eareckson Tada

Character is both developed and revealed by tests, and all of life is a test.

Rick Warren

Character is made in the small moments of our lives.

Phillips Brooks

Maintaining your integrity in a world of sham is no small accomplishment.

Wayne Oates

Image is what people think we are; integrity is what we really are.

John Maxwell

A TIMELY TIP

Never be afraid of praising your husband too much, but be very afraid of praising him too little.

YOUR OWN IDEAS ABOUT:
The Rewards of Being Married to an Honorable Man

_____

_____

_____

_____

_____

_____

_____

_____

_____

_____

_____

_____

_____

_____

"THANK YOU FOR YOUR FORGIVENESS. I WILL ALWAYS FORGIVE YOU, TOO."

*All bitterness, anger and wrath, insult
and slander must be removed from you,
along with all wickedness. And be kind and
compassionate to one another,
forgiving one another,
just as God also forgave you in Christ.*

—

Ephesians 4:31-32 Holman CSB

If you want to make your love last a lifetime, you and your husband must learn the art of forgiveness. Why? Because all of our loved ones are imperfect (as are we). How often must we forgive each other? More times than we can count. In other words, we must not just learn how to forgive; we must learn how to keep forgiving (Matthew 18:21-22).

Perhaps granting forgiveness is hard for you. If so, you are not alone. Granting heartfelt forgiveness is often difficult at times—difficult but not impossible.

When it comes to the hard work of forgiving those who have injured us, God is willing to help, but He expects us to do some of the work—and when we do so, we are blessed.

When we learn the art of forgiveness, we earn peace within our marriages and peace within our hearts. But when we harbor bitterness against others, we forfeit that peace—and by doing so, we bring needless harm to ourselves and to our loved ones. So, if there exists even one person, alive or dead, whom you have not forgiven (and that includes yourself or your husband), follow God's commandment—forgive.

Because bitterness, anger, and regret are emotions that have no place in your life or your marriage.

Hatred stirs up conflicts, but love covers all offenses.

Proverbs 10:12 Holman CSB

A person's insight gives him patience, and his virtue is to overlook an offense.

Proverbs 19:11 Holman CSB

Be merciful, just as your Father also is merciful.

Luke 6:36 Holman CSB

And whenever you stand praying, if you have anything against anyone, forgive him, so that your Father in heaven may also forgive you your wrongdoing.

Mark 11:25 Holman CSB

May mercy, peace, and love be multiplied to you.

Jude 1:2 Holman CSB

More Great Ideas

God calls upon the loved not just to love but to be loving. God calls upon the forgiven not just to forgive but to be forgiving.

Beth Moore

Forgiveness is actually the best revenge because it not only sets us free from the person we forgive, but it frees us to move into all that God has in store for us.

Stormie Omartian

We are products of our past, but we don't have to be prisoners of it. God specializes in giving people a fresh start.

Rick Warren

Miracles broke the physical laws of the universe; forgiveness broke the moral rules.

Philip Yancey

After the forgiving comes laughter, a deeper love—and further opportunities to forgive.

Ruth Bell Graham

The sequence of forgiveness and then repentance, rather than repentance and then forgiveness, is crucial for understanding the gospel of grace.

Brennan Manning

Only the truly forgiven are truly forgiving.

C. S. Lewis

Forgiveness is the precondition of love.

Catherine Marshall

A TIMELY TIP

When your husband becomes angry or upset, you'll tend to become angry and upset, too. Resist that temptation. Keep your cool, even when everybody else is losing theirs! By not fanning the flames, you'll help extinguish the fire.

More from God's Word About Anger

Don't let your spirit rush to be angry, for anger abides in the heart of fools.

Ecclesiastes 7:9 Holman CSB

My dearly loved brothers, understand this: everyone must be quick to hear, slow to speak, and slow to anger, for man's anger does not accomplish God's righteousness.

James 1:19-20 Holman CSB

A fool's displeasure is known at once, but whoever ignores an insult is sensible.

Proverbs 12:16 Holman CSB

All bitterness, anger and wrath, insult and slander must be removed from you, along with all wickedness. And be kind and compassionate to one another, forgiving one another, just as God also forgave you in Christ.

Ephesians 4:31-32 Holman CSB

YOUR OWN IDEAS ABOUT:
The Importance of Forgiveness

_____

_____

_____

_____

_____

_____

_____

_____

_____

_____

_____

_____

_____

_____

_____

_____

_____

_____

_____

"I AM GRATEFUL FOR THE THINGS YOU DO AND THE THINGS WE SHARE."

Let the Word of Christ—the Message— have the run of the house. Give it plenty of room in your lives. Instruct and direct one another using good common sense. And sing, sing your hearts out to God! Let every detail in your lives—words, actions, whatever—be done in the name of the Master, Jesus, thanking God the Father every step of the way.

—

Colossians 3:16-17 MSG

Are you grateful for the things your husband does? Then tell him so. And are you thankful for the things that God has done for you and your family? Then tell Him so, too.

It's important to express gratitude to our families, to our friends, to our spouses, and to our Creator, but sometimes it's hard. After all, for most of us, life is busy and complicated. We have countless responsibilities, some of which begin before sunrise and many of which end long after sunset. Amid the rush and crush of the daily grind, it is easy to lose sight of our blessings. But, when we forget to slow down and say thanks to the ones who have earned it, we do our loved ones a disservice. And if we fail to praise God, we rob ourselves of His presence, His peace, and His joy.

Our task, as Christians, is to praise God many times each day. Then, with gratitude in our hearts, we can face our daily duties with the perspective and power that only He can provide.

Rejoice always, pray without ceasing, in everything give thanks; for this is the will of God in Christ Jesus for you.

1 Thessalonians 5:16-18 NKJV

Therefore as you have received Christ Jesus the Lord, walk in Him, rooted and built up in Him and established in the faith, just as you were taught, and overflowing with thankfulness.

Colossians 2:6-7 Holman CSB

Those who cling to worthless idols forsake faithful love, but as for me, I will sacrifice to You with a voice of thanksgiving. I will fulfill what I have vowed. Salvation is from the Lord!

Jonah 2:8-9 Holman CSB

Thanks be to God for His indescribable gift.

2 Corinthians 9:15 Holman CSB

Give thanks to the Lord, for He is good; His faithful love endures forever.

Psalm 118:29 Holman CSB

MORE GREAT IDEAS

A spirit of thankfulness makes all the difference.

Billy Graham

Nobody who gets enough food and clothing in a world where most are hungry and cold has any business to talk about "misery."

C. S. Lewis

Contentment comes when we develop an attitude of gratitude for the important things we do have in our lives that we tend to take for granted if we have our eyes staring longingly at our neighbor's stuff.

Dave Ramsey

Gratitude changes the pangs of memory into a tranquil joy.

Dietrich Bonhoeffer

A sense of gratitude for God's presence in our lives will help open our eyes to what he has done in the past and what he will do in the future.

Emilie Barnes

Live today fully, expressing gratitude for all you have been, all you are right now, and all you are becoming.

Melodie Beattie

We become happy, spiritually prosperous people not because we receive what we want, but because we appreciate what we have.

Penelope Stokes

If you won't fill your heart with gratitude, the devil will fill it with something else.

Marie T. Freeman

A Timely Tip

Developing an attitude of gratitude is key to a joyful and satisfying life. So ask yourself this question: "Am I grateful enough?"

MORE FROM GOD'S WORD ABOUT CONTENTMENT

I have learned to be content in whatever circumstances I am.

Philippians 4:11 Holman CSB

A tranquil heart is life to the body, but jealousy is rottenness to the bones.

Proverbs 14:30 Holman CSB

The LORD will give strength to His people; the LORD will bless His people with peace.

Psalm 29:11 NKJV

Let your conduct be without covetousness; be content with such things as you have. For He Himself has said, "I will never leave you nor forsake you."

Hebrews 13:5 NKJV

But godliness with contentment is a great gain.

1 Timothy 6:6 Holman CSB

Expressing Your Admiration

A good man produces good things
from his storeroom of good.
Matthew 12:35 Holman CSB

Whether he admits it or not, your husband wants admiration from his kids, from his friends, from his co-workers, and most of all from you. You see, when it comes to praise, most men are like sponges: they have an amazing ability to soak it up. Now, this doesn't mean that your hubby is overly prideful or pridefully sinful; it simply means that he has a healthy need to be admired by you, the most important woman in his life.

Do you tell your husband that you appreciate him, that you admire him, and that you're thankful for all the things he does? And do you tell him these things every day? If so, you already know that he never gets tired of your praise. And that's not surprising because he's living and working in a difficult world, a tough place to make ends meet, a place where he needs every bit of encouragement he can get.

So you do yourself, your family, your marriage, and your husband a favor: express your appreciation and admiration early and often. He needs to hear good things from you, and he needs to hear them now.

Don't speak evil against each other, my dear brothers and sisters. If you criticize each other and condemn each other, then you are criticizing and condemning God's law. But you are not a judge who can decide whether the law is right or wrong. Your job is to obey it.

James 4:11 NLT

Our Father is kind; you be kind. Don't pick on people, jump on their failures, criticize their faults—unless, of course, you want the same treatment. Don't condemn those who are down; that hardness can boomerang. Be easy on people; you'll find life a lot easier.

Luke 6:36-37 MSG

Your Own Ideas About:
Some of the Things You're Most Grateful For

_____

_____

_____

_____

_____

_____

_____

_____

_____

_____

_____

_____

_____

_____

"I WILL BE STRONG FOR YOU."

She is clothed with strength and dignity,
and she laughs with no fear of the future.
When she speaks, her words are wise,
and kindness is the rule when she gives
instructions. She carefully watches all that
goes on in her household and does not have
to bear the consequences of laziness.

—

Proverbs 31:25-27 NLT

These are difficult days, days when husbands and wives need to support and strengthen each other. Many couples are working harder and getting by on less. Sadly, many marriages are being torn apart, but it need not be so.

Building a marriage that can endure tough times requires effort, which is perfectly okay with God. God has created a world in which diligence is rewarded and sloth is not. So, if you sincerely want to build a loving relationship that stands the test of time, you must be willing to work at it. Period.

The work of building a strong marriage requires heaping helpings of consideration, cooperation, self-sacrifice, discipline, empathy, patience, prayer, and perseverance. If that sounds like lots of effort, it is—but the rewards are worth it.

God did not create you to live a mediocre life or to be a mediocre wife. And He does not intend that your marriage be "average." He created you and your husband for far greater things. Reaching for greater things usually requires effort, and so it is with your marriage. Success doesn't come easily, which is just fine with God. After all, He knows that you're up to the task, and He has big plans for you and your marriage. Very big plans.

So stay strong, support your spouse, and trust your Heavenly Father. And while you're at it, please don't forget that when you and your husband work diligently with God, there's nothing, absolutely nothing, that the three of you can't handle.

But those who wait on the Lord shall renew their strength; they shall mount up with wings like eagles, they shall run and not be weary, they shall walk and not faint.

Isaiah 40:31 NKJV

He said unto me, My grace is sufficient for thee: for my strength is made perfect in weakness.

2 Corinthians 12:9 KJV

Whatever your hand finds to do, do it with all your might....

Ecclesiastes 9:10 NIV

The LORD is my strength and my song....

Exodus 15:2 NIV

I can do all things through Him who strengthens me.

Philippians 4:13 NASB

MORE GREAT IDEAS

The same God who empowered Samson, Gideon, and Paul seeks to empower my life and your life, because God hasn't changed.

Bill Hybels

No matter how heavy the burden, daily strength is given, so I expect we need not give ourselves any concern as to what the outcome will be. We must simply go forward.

Annie Armstrong

All the power of God—the same power that hung the stars in place and put the planets in their courses and transformed Earth—now resides in you to energize and strengthen you to become the person God created you to be.

Anne Graham Lotz

A divine strength is given to those who yield themselves to the Father and obey what He tells them to do.

Warren Wiersbe

If we take God's program, we can have God's power—not otherwise.

E. Stanley Jones

God is great and God is powerful, but we must invite him to be powerful in our lives. His strength is always there, but it's up to us to provide a channel through which that power can flow.

Bill Hybels

A TIMELY TIP

Need strength? Slow down, get more rest, engage in sensible exercise, and—most importantly—turn your troubles over to God.

MORE FROM GOD'S WORD ABOUT HOPE

Let us hold on to the confession of our hope without wavering, for He who promised is faithful.

Hebrews 10:23 Holman CSB

For I know the thoughts that I think toward you, says the Lord, thoughts of peace and not of evil, to give you a future and a hope. Then you will call upon Me and go and pray to Me, and I will listen to you.

Jeremiah 29:11-12 NKJV

Hope deferred makes the heart sick.

Proverbs 13:12 NKJV

Sustain me as You promised, and I will live; do not let me be ashamed of my hope.

Psalm 119:116 Holman CSB

Be of good courage, and He shall strengthen your heart, all you who hope in the Lord.

Psalm 31:24 NKJV

YOUR OWN IDEAS ABOUT:
Simple Ways You Can Support Your Husband

_____

_____

_____

_____

_____

_____

_____

_____

_____

_____

_____

_____

_____

_____

_____

_____

_____

"I UNDERSTAND THAT WE ARE ON A SPIRITUAL JOURNEY."

*But grow in the grace and knowledge
of our Lord and Savior Jesus Christ.
To Him be the glory both now
and to the day of eternity.*

—

2 Peter 3:18 Holman CSB

At its best, a Christian marriage is this: a partnership between two believers who embark upon a lifelong journey toward spiritual maturity and growth. No Christian couple should ever be completely satisfied with the condition of their spiritual health; instead, they should continue to grow in the love and the knowledge of their Savior.

When we cease to grow, either emotionally or spiritually, we do ourselves and our loved ones a profound disservice. But, if we study God's Word, if we obey His commandments, and if we live in the center of His will, we will not be stagnant believers; we will, instead, be growing Christians . . . and that's exactly what God wants for our marriages and our lives.

Does your husband encourage your spiritual growth, and is the reverse also true? If so, you are to be congratulated. If not, it's time for change. After all, God doesn't want you (or your marriage) to be stagnant. He wants you to keep growing and growing. And that's exactly what you should want, too.

For this reason also, since the day we heard this, we haven't stopped praying for you. We are asking that you may be filled with the knowledge of His will in all wisdom and spiritual understanding.

Colossians 1:9 Holman CSB

For though by this time you ought to be teachers, you need someone to teach you again the basic principles of God's revelation. You need milk, not solid food. Now everyone who lives on milk is inexperienced with the message about righteousness, because he is an infant. But solid food is for the mature—for those whose senses have been trained to distinguish between good and evil.

Hebrews 5:12-14 Holman CSB

Leave inexperience behind, and you will live; pursue the way of understanding.

Proverbs 9:6 Holman CSB

Like newborn infants, desire the unadulterated spiritual milk, so that you may grow by it in your salvation.

1 Peter 2:2 Holman CSB

More Great Ideas

We've grown to be one soul—two parts; our lives are so intertwined that when some passion stirs your heart, I feel the quake in mine.

Gloria Gaither

Growth takes place in quietness, in hidden ways, in silence and solitude. The process is not accessible to observation.

Eugene Peterson

We often become mentally and spiritually barren because we're so busy.

Franklin Graham

The vigor of our spiritual lives will be in exact proportion to the place held by the Bible in our lives and in our thoughts.

George Mueller

God's plan for our guidance is for us to grow gradually in wisdom before we get to the crossroads.

Bill Hybels

A Christian is never in a state of completion but always in the process of becoming.

Martin Luther

Spiritual growth consists most in the growth of the root, which is out of sight.

Matthew Henry

We look at our burdens and heavy loads, and we shrink from them. But, if we lift them and bind them about our hearts, they become wings, and on them we can rise and soar toward God.

Mrs. Charles E. Cowman

A TIMELY TIP

Today, talk to your husband about the strength that can be yours when you allow Christ to dwell at the center of your marriage.

More from God's Word About Listening to Your Conscience

I always do my best to have a clear conscience toward God and men.

Acts 24:16 Holman CSB

Let us draw near with a true heart in full assurance of faith, our hearts sprinkled clean from an evil conscience and our bodies washed in pure water.

Hebrews 10:22 Holman CSB

I will cling to my righteousness and never let it go. My conscience will not accuse [me] as long as I live!

Job 27:6 Holman CSB

Do not be conformed to this age, but be transformed by the renewing of your mind, so that you may discern what is the good, pleasing, and perfect will of God.

Romans 12:2 Holman CSB

God, create a clean heart for me and renew a steadfast spirit within me.

Psalm 51:10 Holman CSB

YOUR OWN IDEAS ABOUT:
The Rewards That Can Be Yours If You Keep Growing Spiritually

_____

_____

_____

_____

_____

_____

_____

_____

_____

_____

_____

_____

_____

_____

"I WILL MAKE OUR HOME A HAPPY PLACE."

*A house is built by wisdom,
and it is established by understanding;
by knowledge the rooms are filled with
every precious and beautiful treasure.*

—

Proverbs 24:3-4 Holman CSB

Are you determined to make your home a happy, peaceful place? Hopefully so because that's what your family wants, that's what your husband wants, and that's what God wants, too.

For Christian couples, kindness is not an option; it is a commandment. Jesus teaches, "In everything, therefore, treat people the same way you want them to treat you, for this is the Law and the Prophets" (Matthew 7:12 NASB). Jesus did not say, "In some things, treat people as you wish to be treated." And, He did not say, "From time to time, treat others with kindness." Christ said that we should treat others as we wish to be treated in everything. This, of course, isn't always easy, but as Christians, we are commanded to do our best.

Healthy marriages are built upon the Golden Rule. Healthy marriages are built upon sharing and caring, two principles that are found time and time again in God's Holy Word. When we read God's Word and follow His commandments, we enrich our own lives and the lives of those who are closest to us.

Today, as you consider all the things that Christ has done in your life, honor Him by being a little kinder than necessary. Honor Him by slowing down long enough to say an extra word of encouragement to your loved ones. Honor Him by obeying the Golden Rule. He expects no less; He deserves no less. And so, by the way, does your husband.

Choose for yourselves today the one you will worship . . . . As for me and my family, we will worship the Lord.

—

Joshua 24:15 Holman CSB

The Lord's curse is on the household of the wicked, but He blesses the home of the righteous; He mocks those who mock, but gives grace to the humble. The wise will inherit honor, but He holds up fools to dishonor.

Proverbs 3:33-35 Holman CSB

Unless the Lord builds a house, the work of the builders is useless.

Psalm 127:1 NLT

It takes knowledge to fill a home with rare and beautiful treasures.

Proverbs 24:4 NCV

Hear, O Israel: The LORD our God, the LORD is one. Love the LORD your God with all your heart and with all your soul and with all your strength. These commandments that I give you today are to be upon your hearts. Impress them on your children. Talk about them when you sit at home and when you walk along the road, when you lie down and when you get up.

Deuteronomy 6:4-7 NIV

MORE GREAT IDEAS

The secret of a happy home life is that the members of the family learn to give and receive love.

Billy Graham

Home is not only where the heart is; it is also where the happiness is.

Marie T. Freeman

Whatever else may be said about the home, it is the bottom line of life, the anvil upon which attitudes and convictions are hammered out.

Charles Swindoll

The home should be a kind of church, a place where God is honored.

Billy Graham

God, give us Christian homes! Homes where the Bible is loved and taught, homes where the Master's will is sought.

B. B. McKinney

To go home is to be refreshed in my spirit and refocused in my thoughts and renewed in my strength and restored in my heart.

Anne Graham Lotz

God's peace is like a river, not a pond. In other words, a sense of health and well-being, both of which are expressions of the Hebrew shalom, can permeate our homes even when we're in white-water rapids.

Beth Moore

A Timely Tip

Make your home a sanctuary, a place filled with love and laughter.

Making Time for Your Marriage

*To everything there is a season,
a time for every purpose under heaven.*
Ecclesiastes 3:1 NKJV

If you sincerely want your marriage to flourish, then you should be prepared to invest the time and energy required to do so. Wise couples invest time—high quality time—nurturing their relationships. And it shows.

Time is a precious, nonrenewable gift from God. But sometimes, we treat our time here on earth as if it were not a gift at all: We may be tempted to squander time in countless ways, and when we do so, we pay a high price for our mistaken priorities.

How are you choosing to spend the time that God has given you? Are you carving out large blocks of time to spend with your husband? Or are you rushing through the day with scarcely a moment to spare?

As you establish priorities for your day and your life, remember that each new day is a special treasure to be savored and celebrated with your loved ones. As a Christian couple, you and your husband have much to celebrate and much to do. It's up to both of you to honor God for the gift of time by using that gift wisely . . . and using it together.

Your Own Ideas About:
Simple Ways You Can Make Your Home a Little
More Peaceful

_____

_____

_____

_____

_____

_____

_____

_____

_____

_____

_____

_____

_____

"I WILL NEVER STOP LOVING YOU."

So we must not get tired of doing good,
for we will reap at the proper time
if we don't give up.

—

Galatians 6:9 Holman CSB

Your husband needs to know that you love him today, that you will love him tomorrow, and that you will love him forever. Marriage is, after all, a marathon, not a sprint—and couples who expect otherwise will be sadly disappointed. That's why husbands and wives need large quantities of patience, forgiveness, hope, and perseverance.

Every marriage and every life has its share of roadblocks and stumbling blocks; these situations require courage and determination. As an example of perfect courage and steadfast determination, we need look no further than our Savior, Jesus Christ.

Jesus finished what He began. Despite the torture He endured, despite the shame of the cross, Jesus was steadfast in His faithfulness to God. We, too, must remain faithful—faithful to God, faithful to our principles, and faithful to our loved ones—especially during times of transition or hardship.

The next time you are tempted to give up on yourself, your duties, or your relationships, ask yourself this question: "What would Jesus have me do?" When you find the answer to that question, you'll know precisely what to do.

Do you not know that the runners in a stadium all race, but only one receives the prize? Run in such a way that you may win. Now everyone who competes exercises self-control in everything. However, they do it to receive a perishable crown, but we an imperishable one.

1 Corinthians 9:24-25 Holman CSB

Let us lay aside every weight and the sin that so easily ensnares us, and run with endurance the race that lies before us, keeping our eyes on Jesus, the source and perfecter of our faith.

Hebrews 12:1-2 Holman CSB

Now we want each of you to demonstrate the same diligence for the final realization of your hope, so that you won't become lazy, but imitators of those who inherit the promises through faith and perseverance.

Hebrews 6:11-12 Holman CSB

For you have need of endurance, so that after you have done the will of God, you may receive the promise.

Hebrews 10:36 NKJV

MORE GREAT IDEAS

In the Bible, patience is not a passive acceptance of circumstances. It is a courageous perseverance in the face of suffering and difficulty.

Warren Wiersbe

Achievers refused to hold on to the common excuses for failure. They turned their stumbling blocks into stepping stones. They realized that they couldn't determine every circumstance in life but they could determine their choice of attitude towards every circumstance.

John Maxwell

Love is a steady wish for the loved person's ultimate good.

C. S. Lewis

Failure is one of life's most powerful teachers. How we handle our failures determines whether we're going to simply "get by" in life or "press on."

Beth Moore

In all negotiations of difficulties, a man may not look to sow and reap at once. He must prepare his business and so ripen it by degrees.

Francis Bacon

Jesus taught that perseverance is the essential element in prayer.

E. M. Bounds

Every achievement worth remembering is stained with the blood of diligence and scarred by the wounds of disappointment.

Charles Swindoll

A TIMELY TIP

Remember the words of Winston Churchill: He's the wise man who said, "Never give in; never give in; never give in." If Churchill hadn't been the Prime Minister of England, he would have made a pretty good marriage counselor.

YOUR OWN IDEAS ABOUT:
The Power of Perseverance

_____

_____

_____

_____

_____

_____

_____

_____

_____

_____

_____

_____

_____

_____

_____

_____

"I UNDERSTAND THE IMPORTANCE OF COOPERATION."

If a kingdom is divided against itself,
that kingdom cannot stand.
If a house is divided against itself,
that house cannot stand.

—

Mark 3:24-25 Holman CSB

Have you and your husband learned the fine art of cooperation? And do you remind him every day that you're ready, willing, and able to help him get things done? If so, you have learned the wisdom of "give and take," not the foolishness of "me first."

Cooperation is the art of compromising on little things while keeping your eye on the big thing: your relationship.

Cooperative relationships grow and flourish over time. But, when couples fail to cooperate, they unintentionally sow seeds of dissatisfaction and disharmony.

If you're like most of us, you're probably a little bit headstrong: you probably want most things done in a fashion resembling the popular song "My Way." But, if you are observant, you will notice that those people who always insist upon "my way or the highway" usually end up with "the highway."

A better strategy for all concerned is to abandon the search for "my way" and search instead for "our way." That tune has a far happier ending. So today, tell your husband that you're serious about being a cooperative, solution-oriented wife, a woman who's fully prepared to do her fair share, and then some. He needs to hear those words from you. Now.

Blessed are the peacemakers . . . .

Matthew 5:9 Holman CSB

Carry one another's burdens; in this way you will fulfill the law of Christ.

Galatians 6:2 Holman CSB

Pursue peace with everyone, and holiness—without it no one will see the Lord.

Hebrews 12:14 Holman CSB

Two are better than one because they have a good reward for their efforts. For if either falls, his companion can lift him up; but pity the one who falls without another to lift him up.

Ecclesiastes 4:9-10 Holman CSB

MORE GREAT IDEAS

In the bond of marriage, we are to stand at the altar of Sacrifice or we're not to stand at all.

Beth Moore

Being committed to one's mate is not a matter of demanding rights, but a matter of releasing rights.

Charles Swindoll

There is nothing wrong with a marriage that sacrifice wouldn't heal.

Elisabeth Elliot

Selfishness and marriage don't mix.

Marie T. Freeman

Husbands and wives who live happily ever after learn to give and take and to reach agreement by mutual consent. A man or woman with an unmovable backbone is in real trouble. God made backbones that can stand rigid but can also bend when necessary.

Vance Havner

A Christians wife's responsibility balances delicately between knowing when to submit and when to outwit. Adapting to our husbands never implies the annihilation of our creativity, rather the blossoming of it.

Ruth Bell Graham

There is no such thing as a no-maintenance marriage, but energy and time devoted to this holy enterprise will reap lasting, valuable dividends every time.

Ed Young

Cooperation is a two-way street, but for too many couples, it's the road less traveled.

Marie T. Freeman

A TIMELY TIP

Be cooperative. Remember that the two of you are in this thing together, so play like teammates, not rivals.

He Needs Your Help

A virtuous woman is a crown to her husband . . . .
Proverbs 12:4 KJV

Your husband needs your help, but sometimes he may be too proud, or too stubborn, to ask for it. In a misguided effort to cast himself in the role of "the strong, silent type," he may be holding his feelings inside. Or he may be laboring under the misconception that he should try to fix everything by himself. Yet you know that you're willing (and perfectly able) to help. And you should tell him so.

These are difficult times, times when many families must work harder and longer to make ends meet. Your husband needs to know that you're totally supportive, that you're completely cooperative, that you're eager to listen, and that you're trying hard to understand his needs.

When work needs to be done, wise wives stay strong, and so should you. Your job is to make certain your husband knows you're always able and ready to help. It's an enormously important role that only you can fill.

Let them first learn to show piety at home and to repay their parents; for this is good and acceptable before God.

1 Timothy 5:4 NKJV

Love must be without hypocrisy. Detest evil; cling to what is good. Show family affection to one another with brotherly love. Outdo one another in showing honor.

Romans 12:9–10 Holman CSB

If a kingdom is divided against itself, that kingdom cannot stand. If a house is divided against itself, that house cannot stand.

Mark 3:24-25 Holman CSB

Now if anyone does not provide for his own relatives, and especially for his household, he has denied the faith and is worse than an unbeliever.

1 Timothy 5:8 Holman CSB

Your Own Ideas About:
The Importance of Cooperation within Your Marriage

_____

_____

_____

_____

_____

_____

_____

_____

_____

_____

_____

_____

_____

_____

_____

"I TRUST GOD WITH MY LIFE, AND I TRUST HIM WITH OUR MARRIAGE."

*It is better to take refuge
in the Lord than to trust in man.*

—

Psalm 118:8 Holman CSB

D o you trust God to rule over your life and your marriage? Unless you can answer this question with a resounding yes, you and your husband still have some spiritual growing up to do.

God loves you. Period. He loves you more than you can imagine; His affection is deeper and more profound than you can fathom. God made you in His own image and gave you salvation through the person of His Son Jesus Christ. And now, precisely because you are a wondrous creation treasured by God, a crucial question presents itself: What will you do in response to God's love? Will you ignore it or embrace it? Will you return it or neglect it? Will you deny it, or will you share it? These decisions, of course, are yours and yours alone.

When you learn to trust God completely, you are forever changed. When you turn the future over to Him, you feel differently about yourself, about your loved ones, about your marriage, and about your world. When you embrace God's love, you find new ways to share His message—and His mercy—with others.

Have you built every aspect of your life—including your marriage—upon the firm foundation of God's unwavering love for you and yours? Do you trust Him completely and without reservation? If so, you have built your life on the Rock that cannot be moved. And, you have accepted a priceless gift that is yours to share and to keep . . . now and throughout all eternity.

For the Lord God is a sun and shield. The Lord gives grace and glory; He does not withhold the good from those who live with integrity. Lord of Hosts, happy is the person who trusts in You!

Psalm 84:11-12 Holman CSB

The LORD is my rock, and my fortress, and my deliverer; my God, my strength, in whom I will trust....

Psalm 18:2 KJV

MORE GREAT IDEAS

God delights to meet the faith of one who looks up to Him and says, "Lord, You know that I cannot do this—but I believe that You can!"

Amy Carmichael

It helps to resign as the controller of your fate. All that energy we expend to keep things running right is not what keeps things running right.

Anne Lamott

Are you serious about wanting God's guidance to become the person he wants you to be? The first step is to tell God that you know you can't manage your own life; that you need his help.

Catherine Marshall

The more we learn to receive and depend upon His grace in deepening measure, the less anxious we will be about what the future holds.

Cynthia Heald

Brother, is your faith looking upward today? / Trust in the promise of the Savior. / Sister, is the light shining bright on your way? / Trust in the promise of thy Lord.

Fanny Crosby

Do not be afraid, then, that if you trust, or tell others to trust, the matter will end there. Trust is only the beginning and the continual foundation. When we trust Him, the Lord works, and His work is the important part of the whole matter.

Hannah Whitall Smith

A TIMELY TIP

One of the most important lessons that you can ever learn is to trust God for everything, and that includes timing. In other words, you should trust God to decide the best time for things to happen. Sometimes it's hard to trust God, but it's always the right thing to do.

Your Own Ideas About:
Ways That God Has Blessed Your Family

_____

_____

_____

_____

_____

_____

_____

_____

_____

_____

_____

_____

_____

_____

_____

_____

"I PRAISE GOD FOR YOU AND FOR OUR MARRIAGE."

*It is good to give thanks to the Lord,
and to sing praises to Your name,
O Most High; to declare Your
lovingkindness in the morning,
and Your faithfulness every night.*

—

Psalm 92:1-2 NKJV

I t's easy to "compartmentalize" our waking hours into a few familiar categories: work, rest, play, family time, and worship. As creatures of habit, we may find ourselves praising God only at particular times of the day or on a particular day of the week. But praise for our Creator should never be reserved for mealtimes, or bedtimes, or church. Instead, we should praise God all day, every day, to the greatest extent we can, with thanksgiving in our hearts, and with a song on our lips.

Worship and praise should be woven into the fabric of everything we do; they should not be relegated to a weekly three-hour visit to church on Sunday morning. A. W. Tozer correctly observed, "If you will not worship God seven days a week, you do not worship Him on one day a week."

Do you praise God many times each day? And do you thank Him specifically for your husband and your family? If so, keep up the good work; if not, it's time to reassess your priorities. When you consider the wonderful things that God has done for you, you'll find the time—or more accurately you'll make the time—to praise Him for all that He has done.

Every time you notice a gift from the Creator, thank Him and praise Him. His works are marvelous, His gifts are beyond understanding, and His love endures forever.

Praise the Lord, all nations! Glorify Him, all peoples! For great is His faithful love to us; the Lord's faithfulness endures forever. Hallelujah!

Psalm 117 Holman CSB

I will praise the Lord at all times, I will constantly speak his praises.

Psalm 34:1 NLT

Through Him then, let us continually offer up a sacrifice of praise to God, that is, the fruit of lips that give thanks to His name.

Hebrews 13:15 NASB

MORE GREAT IDEAS

Words fail to express my love for this holy Book, my gratitude for its author, for His love and goodness. How shall I thank him for it?

Lottie Moon

A child of God should be a visible beatitude for joy and a living doxology for gratitude.

C. H. Spurgeon

The time for universal praise is sure to come some day. Let us begin to do our part now.

Hannah Whitall Smith

Nothing we do is more powerful or more life-changing than praising God.

Stormie Omartian

Our God is the sovereign Creator of the universe! He loves us as His own children and has provided every good thing we have; He is worthy of our praise every moment.

Shirley Dobson

Holy, holy, holy! Lord God Almighty! All Thy works shall praise Thy name in earth, and sky, and sea.

Reginald Heber

Praise is the highest occupation of any being.

Max Lucado

Praise reestablishes the proper chain of command; we recognize that the King is on the throne and that he has saved his people.

Max Lucado

A TIMELY TIP

Remember that it always pays to praise your Creator. That's why thoughtful believers (like you) make it a habit to carve out quiet moments throughout the day to praise God.

YOUR OWN IDEAS ABOUT:
The Rewards of Praising God

_____

_____

_____

_____

_____

_____

_____

_____

_____

_____

_____

_____

_____

_____

"I TREASURE OUR FAMILY."

Choose for yourselves today the one you will worship . . . . As for me and my family, we will worship the Lord.

—

Joshua 24:15 Holman CSB

As a thoughtful wife, you know that your family is a priceless treasure from God. And if you're a wise wife, you'll make certain that your husband knows that you know. How? By telling him how thankful you are for the gift of family, that's how.

But sometimes, you'll be tempted to rush through life while giving little notice to your blessings. After all, if you're a busy woman working in a demanding world, the pressures can be intense. Raising a family is a big job, but with God's help, you're up to the task.

When you place God squarely in the center of your family's life—when you worship Him, praise Him, trust Him, and love Him—then He will most certainly bless you and yours in ways that you could have scarcely imagined.

So the next time your family life becomes a little stressful, remember this: That little band of men, women, kids, and babies is a priceless treasure on temporary loan from the Father above. And it's your responsibility to praise God for that gift—and to act accordingly.

If a kingdom is divided against itself, that kingdom cannot stand. If a house is divided against itself, that house cannot stand.

Mark 3:24-25 Holman CSB

The one who brings ruin on his household will inherit the wind.

Proverbs 11:29 Holman CSB

Unless the Lord builds a house, its builders labor over it in vain; unless the Lord watches over a city, the watchman stays alert in vain.

Psalm 127:1 HSCB

Love must be without hypocrisy. Detest evil; cling to what is good. Show family affection to one another with brotherly love. Outdo one another in showing honor.

Romans 12:9-10 Holman CSB

MORE GREAT IDEAS

Homes that are built on anything other than love are bound to crumble.

Billy Graham

The only true source of meaning in life is found in love for God and his son Jesus Christ, and love for mankind, beginning with our own families.

James Dobson

There is so much compassion and understanding that is gained when we've experienced God's grace firsthand within our own families.

Lisa Whelchel

A home is a place where we find direction.

Gigi Graham Tchividjian

Calm and peaceful, the home should be the one place where people are certain they will be welcomed, received, protected, and loved.

Ed Young

Love is most often found in the home—in the presence of a caring and considerate mate who nurtures love daily.

Zig Ziglar

More than any other single factor in a person's formative years, family life forges character.

John Maxwell

Every Christian family ought to be, as it were, a little church, consecrated to Christ, and wholly influenced and governed by His rules.

Jonathan Edwards

A TIMELY TIP

Today, think about the importance of saying "yes" to your family even if it means saying "no" to other obligations.

SETTING THE RIGHT KIND OF EXAMPLE

Be an example to the believers in word, in conduct, in love, in spirit, in faith, in purity.
1 Timothy 4:12 NKJV

Whether you and your husband realize it or not, your marriage serves as a powerful example to family and friends. So here's the big question: what kind of example is your marriage? Is yours a marriage that honors God? Is it a marriage that strengthens the bonds of family? Is it a marriage that others should seek to emulate? If so, you are fortunate, you are wise, and you are blessed.

We live in cynical, temptation-filled world where negative role models abound and positive role models are often in short supply. That's why your positive role model is so important. When you and your husband serve as positive examples for other couples, you are helping those couples visualize positive changes that they can make in their own marriages.

Phillips Brooks advised, "Be such a person, and live such a life, that if every person were such as you, and every life a life like yours, this earth would be God's Paradise." And that's sound advice because our families and friends are watching . . . and so is God.

Set an example of good works yourself, with integrity and dignity in your teaching.

Titus 2:7 Holman CSB

Do all things without complaining and disputing, that you may become blameless and harmless, children of God without fault in the midst of a crooked and perverse generation, among whom you shine as lights in the world.

Philippians 2:14-15 NKJV

If I take care of my character, my reputation will take care of itself.

D. L. Moody

Your Own Ideas About:
God's Gift to You: Your Family

_____

_____

_____

_____

_____

_____

_____

_____

_____

_____

_____

_____

_____

_____

_____

_____

"OUR LOVE WILL LAST FOREVER."

Love never ends.

—

1 Corinthians 13:8 Holman CSB

The Bible makes it clear that God's love for you and your husband is deeper and more profound than either of you can imagine.

When you and your spouse embrace God together, both of you are forever changed. When you embrace God's love, you feel differently about yourself, your marriage, your family, and your world. When you join together and accept God's love, the two of you will be transformed.

So, if you and your husband genuinely want to build a love that endures, make God the focus of your marriage. When you do, your marriage will last forever—and so will your love.

In a little while the world will see Me no longer, but you will see Me. Because I live, you will live too.

—

John 14:19 Holman CSB

For God loved the world in this way: He gave His only Son, so that everyone who believes in Him will not perish but have eternal life.

John 3:16 Holman CSB

And this is the testimony: God has given us eternal life, and this life is in His Son. The one who has the Son has life. The one who doesn't have the Son of God does not have life.

1 John 5:11-12 Holman CSB

Pursue righteousness, godliness, faith, love, endurance, and gentleness. Fight the good fight for the faith; take hold of eternal life, to which you were called and have made a good confession before many witnesses.

1 Timothy 6:11-12 Holman CSB

Jesus said to her, "I am the resurrection and the life. The one who believes in Me, even if he dies, will live. Everyone who lives and believes in Me will never die—ever. Do you believe this?"

John 11:25-26 Holman CSB

MORE GREAT IDEAS

Love simply cannot spring up without that self-surrender to each other. If either withholds the self, love cannot exist.

E. Stanley Jones

Life without love is empty and meaningless no matter how gifted we are.

Charles Stanley

To have fallen in love hints to our hearts that all of earthly life is not hopelessly fallen. Love is the laughter of God.

Beth Moore

The whole being of any Christian is Faith and Love. Faith brings the man to God; love brings him to men.

Martin Luther

Life is immortal, love eternal; death is nothing but a horizon, and a horizon is only the limit of our vision.

Corrie ten Boom

If you are a believer, your judgment will not determine your eternal destiny. Christ's finished work on Calvary was applied to you the moment you accepted Christ as Savior.

Beth Moore

I can still hardly believe it. I, with shriveled, bent fingers, atrophied muscles, gnarled knees, and no feeling from the shoulders down, will one day have a new body—light, bright and clothed in righteousness—powerful and dazzling.

Joni Eareckson Tada

Once a man is united to God, how could he not live forever? Once a man is separated from God, what can he do but wither and die?

C. S. Lewis

A TIMELY TIP

The ultimate choice is your choice to welcome God's Son into your heart and by doing so accept the gift of eternal life. If you or your husband haven't already done so, make that choice today.

Your Own Ideas About:
What the Gift of Eternal Life Means to You and
Your Husband

_____

_____

_____

_____

_____

_____

_____

_____

_____

_____

_____

_____

_____

_____